SPIRITLED WOMAN BIBLE STUDY: RUTH

Dr. Fuchsia Pickett

SpiritLed Woman Bible Study: Ruth by Fuchsia Pickett
Published by Creation House
Strang Communications Company
600 Rinehart Road
Lake Mary, Florida 32746
Web site: http://www.creationhouse.com

Unless otherwise noted, all Scripture quotations are from the King James Version of the Bible.

Scripture quotations marked NAS are from the New American Standard Bible. Copyright © 1960, 1962, 1963, 1968, 1971, 1972, 1973, 1975, 1977 by the Lockman Foundation. Used by permission.

Library of Congress Catalog Card Number: 98-94937
International Standard Book Number: 0-88419-585-6

9 0 1 2 3 4 5 6 RRD 8 7 6 5 4 3 2 1
Printed in the United States of America

Contents

Introduction

Welcome to The SpiritLed Woman Bible Study Series. This particular study guide from the series is a study of the biblical Book of Ruth. The purpose of this study is to illuminate the stream of revelation flowing as an allegory from the biblical account of this historical love story that is pivotal in the genealogy of the house of David and, subsequently, of Jesus Christ.

The primary thrust of this study guide will focus on Ruth as a prophetic message foreshadowing the coming of Jesus and the restoration of the church. Through allegory and type, we will explore deep truths concerning our relationship with God both as individuals and corporately, and His plan for the church. As you complete this study guide, identify with Ruth as she chooses to enter into relationship with God's people and ultimately with Boaz, who typifies Jesus Christ, the heavenly Bridegroom.

Key teachings explored in Ruth include the implications of spiritual famine and discipline in the life of the believer; the power of choice; the requirement of waiting; and the processes of maturity, grace, obedience, and redemption. These truths are related to the church age and the End-Time ingathering of the harvest through global revival.

Objectives of This Bible Study

The SpiritLed Woman Bible Study Series contains three study guides, each twelve chapters long. It is designed to inspire women to study the Bible—alone or in groups. These booklets are ideal for group study and, at twelve chapters each, would work well as quarterly studies. With the addition of Fuchsia Pickett's *How to Search the Scriptures*—an in-depth book that teaches how to study and interpret the Word of God—as an additional study book, an entire year of study could be accomplished. The series includes study booklets on *Esther,* a study guide covering the historical importance of this brave woman's call "for such a time as this"; *Deborah,* the fascinating historical account of one woman who obeyed the Spirit of God, leading a nation and becoming a deliverer for the people of God; and *Ruth,* this study that you are about to begin.

The goals for this study of Ruth are:

1. To recognize the *allegorical streams* running throughout the Scriptures in general and throughout the Book of Ruth in particular.
2. To examine the causes of *spiritual famine.*
3. To appreciate the *disciplining hand of God* in bringing us to redemption.

4. To comprehend the awesome *power of choice* given to every individual and its role in believers possessing their inheritance in God.
5. To recognize *obedience* as the prerequisite for revelation and rest in God.
6. To rejoice in the realization of the work of Jesus as our *Kinsman-Redeemer.*

To complete this study, you will want to have available for use a King James Version of the Bible and two other translations of the Bible of your choosing. You may also want to purchase a copy of *The Prophetic Romance* by Fuchsia Pickett, which expands on the revelations contained in this study course. Portions of *The Prophetic Romance* have been quoted in this study course. These portions of text can be identified by the asterisk (*) immediately following the quoted text.

As you proceed with this study, may the revelations contained in this prophetic love story change your life and your relationship with your heavenly Bridegroom for eternity.

1

History of Redemption

Tucked away among the massive history books of the Old Testament is the little Book of Ruth, one of the most beautiful, historical love stories of all time. Its authentic historical account of a Jewish family's life rightfully places it with the history books in the canon of Scripture. However, after careful study we must conclude that the Book of Ruth is more than an interesting and inspired book of history. It is "*His*tory"—the story of Christ—for Christ Himself is clearly foreshadowed in this little book.*

In the broadest sense, all of history can be characterized as *His*tory: All events of the human race are evaluated on the basis of whether Christ, the revelation of God to man, was accepted or rejected. *History* is therefore the study of mankind, whom God made for the purpose of fellowshiping with Himself. The *Bible* is the greatest history book ever written; all Scriptures should be studied expecting to see Christ revealed.

- The Old Testament reveals Christ through types and shadows.
- The Gospels reveal Christ as the Son of God, dealing with men.
- The New Testament reveals Christ as the Head of the church.
- The Book of Revelation reveals Christ's reign as King of kings.

The Book of Ruth reveals eternal truths that foreshadow the revelation of the church and explain the "processes" the church must experience in preparation for relationship with Christ. The concept of a woman foreshadowing the church is not strange to students of the Bible. In the New Testament, the church is referred to in the feminine gender. *Ekklesia,* meaning "called-out ones," carries a feminine ending. The church is also referred to as the "bride of Christ."*

Q: *Read Isaiah 54:5–6. In these verses, what relationship does the Word use to explain Christ's relationship to the believer?*

____

Q: *In Ephesians 5:25–33 the church is called:*

____.

> *Q: Read these verses and write a description of Christ's relationship to His bride as revealed in this passage.*

Foundation for Studying Type and Allegory in the Scriptures

Type is a person, thing, or event that represents another, especially another that is to come in the future. *Typology* is the study of types. *Allegory* is a story in which people, things, and happenings have a symbolic significance, not merely a literal one, that is often morally instructive.

Many examples of types and allegories are purposefully used in Scripture. These include:

- The parables of Jesus
- The shepherd psalms of David
- The animal sacrifices of the Old Testament

> *Q: Read Matthew 18:12–14. How is this parable a type of Christ?*

> *Q: Read Psalm 23. What word pictures in this psalm can be used to reveal the nature of God?*

____

____

> *Q: How do the animal sacrifices in the Old Testament foreshadow Christ's atoning work?*

____

____

Three Major Types Running Throughout Scripture

Type	Fulfillment
The tabernacle or temple	New Testament Christians (1 Cor. 3:16)
The human body or anatomy	The body of Christ in the earth (1 Cor. 12:18, 27)
The bride and bridegroom: Rebekah and Isaac, Ruth and Boaz, Esther and the king	The church prepared as a bride for Jesus Christ.

Principles for Understanding Scriptural Type and Allegory

1. Do not attempt to make every word in a story fit a divine truth.
2. The truth a type or allegory teaches must completely agree with God's eternal plan

of salvation for mankind—the shedding of Jesus' blood on Calvary.

Only as types and allegories help us to apply truth to our lives and only as they agree with all other Scripture are they valid revelation. The ultimate purpose for all revelation must be to transform us into the image of Christ.*

Ruth and Numerology

The Book of Ruth is the eighth book in the Bible. In the study of numerology, numbers play a significant role in revealing the plan of redemption. The number *eight* in the Scriptures represents *new beginnings.* For example, Noah was the eighth person saved in the flood (2 Pet. 2:5). Christ taught eight beatitudes (Matt. 5:1–10). And Christ rose from the dead on the "eighth day." (Christ arose on the first day of the week, the eighth day, giving mankind its greatest beginning.)*

Ruth in Context of the Canon of Scriptures

In the study of Scripture we must be careful not to make a single verse stand on its own without relating to its context and relationship to other Scriptures. The books of the Bible are related to the whole of Scripture according to their placement in the canon. The books surrounding Ruth, the book of redemption, are:

- *Genesis*—the book of beginnings
- *Exodus*—the book of redemption

- *Leviticus*—the book of worship
- *Numbers*—the book of warfare
- *Deuteronomy*—the book of obedience
- *Joshua*—the book of possessions
- *Judges*—the book of failure
- *1 and 2 Samuel*—the books of the kingdom

Significance of the "Little Books" of Scripture

The little books of the Bible should not seem insignificant because of their smallness. Each reveals divine truth that will impact our lives for eternity. The following books demonstrate their impact:

- *Obadiah* presents a challenging vision.
- *Esther* foreshadows the personal relationship of the true worshiper of God.
- *Philemon* is a beautiful picture of redemption.
- *Jude* is packed with revelation of the seven steps to apostasy.

The Book of Ruth is one of those powerful little books that reveal to us allegorically what is involved in our own personal redemption as well as that of the body of Christ corporately. Not only Ruth's circumstances, but her attitudes, desires, and decisions relating to those circumstances speak eternal truths on which the restoration of all the blessings of God for our lives depend. Other characters in the narrative teach us by example as well, mirroring the consequences of our own choices and attitudes and helping us to evaluate our relationships with God.*

Q: *Read one of the little books mentioned above. What revelatory knowledge did God make known to you as you read?*

2

Significant Titles in Redemption's Plan

Old Testament names often *revealed one's character prophetically.* For example, Jacob's name means "supplanter and cheater." Those qualities characterized his life as he sought to take the blessing of God from his brother.*

In some instances, names were given to *mark an event in history.* When the glory of God departed from the house of Israel while the wife of the priest was giving birth, she named her son Ichabod, which means "the glory has departed" (1 Sam. 4:21).*

Names were changed for specific reasons, especially when one had an encounter with God. When God established the covenant with Abram, He changed Abram's name to *Abraham.**

> **Q:** *Beside each name listed below give its meaning. Then decide if the name reveals that person's character prophetically, marks an event in history, or is a name that was changed for a specific reason.*

Simon/Peter ______________________________

____

Moses ______________________________

____

Lo-Ruhamah (Hosea's daughter) ______________________________

____

Saul/Paul ______________________________

____

David ______________________________

____

Three Ways God Reveals Himself in Scripture

God reveals Himself to us in the Scriptures in three ways.

Through the names of God

There are over three hundred fifty names of God in the Bible. Each one reveals a wonderful aspect of His nature.

Q: *What characteristic of the nature of God do each of the following names reveal?*

Jehovah-Jireh ______________________

Jehovah-Nissi ______________________

Jehovah-Shalom ______________________

Jehovah-Shammah ______________________

Jehovah-Rophe ______________________

Through the acts of God

God reveals Himself through His acts. We learn what the power of God is like as we read of God dividing the waters, raising the dead, and stilling the storms.*

Through the descriptions of God

Jesus, as the express image of the Father, reveals God in everything He did.

The Book of Ruth

- A well-written, divinely inspired story
- An accurate historical account of events
- An allegory of things to come

Names and Characters in Ruth

The biblical names and characters in the Book of Ruth are filled with prophetic revelation. We will miss much of the significance of the story from God's viewpoint if we do not understand the names. Reading Ruth from an earthly viewpoint gives us factual historical information. Reading it from God's perspective helps us to understand the heavenly truths God wants to communicate to us.*

- *Bethlehem*—"House of Bread" (Ruth 1:1)
- *Judah*—"a place where people praise God" (1:1)
- *Bethlehem-Judah*—"a place of bountiful provision and joy" (1:1)
- *Elimelech* (husband of Naomi)—"God is King" (1:2)
- *Naomi*—"pleasant" (1:2)
- *Mahlon* (their son)—"joy" (1:2)
- *Chilion* (their son)—"song" (1:2)

The above family is a type of the Christian walk as God intends it to be: a house of bread and a place of praise.

> Q: *In the paragraph below, fill in the blanks by adding each of the definitions given above.*

As the redeemed church, God intends for our lives to be characterized as a ____________ and a ____________. Our lives as the temples of the Holy Spirit are to be a ____________. We must recognize __________, and His __________ Spirit will fill our lives continually. Then we will be filled with a __________ of __________ as we worship together in God's house.

[Answers to above blanks: 1) house of bread; 2) a place where people praise God; 3) a place of bountiful provision and joy; 4) God is King; 5) pleasant; 6) song, 7) joy.]

***Special Significance of the Name* Naomi**

The meaning of Naomi's name, "pleasant," carries allegorical significance as it relates to the Scriptures. The Scriptures teach that the knowledge of God is pleasant.*

> When wisdom entereth into thine heart, and knowledge is pleasant unto thy soul; discretion shall preserve thee, understanding shall keep thee.
>
> —PROVERBS 2:10–11

> Her ways are paths of pleasantness, and all her paths are peace.
>
> —PROVERBS 3:17

Naomi is a type of the present church age. We can observe God's initiation and completion of restoration foreshadowed in this eighth book of the Old Testament. As we study further, we will recognize Boaz as a type of Christ, displaying redemptive love through self-sacrifice.

3

Famine's Tragedy: A Cry for Redemption

The happy lifestsyle Naomi and her family enjoyed in Bethlehem-Judah had deteriorated to the devastating circumstances in Moab. As she faced the stark reality of her situation, Naomi must have cried out in desperation, "How could this have happened to me?"*

> And Elimelech Naomi's husband died; and she was left, and her two sons. And they took them wives of the women of Moab; the name of the one was Orpah, and the name of the other Ruth: and they dwelled there about ten years. And Mahlon and Chilion died also both of them; and the woman was left of her two sons and her husband.
>
> —RUTH 1:3–5

Moab is a type of the carnal life, the self-life of the believer. *Egypt* is a type of the believer's sinful life before salvation. Moab, a place of carnality, resulted in the terrible loss of the presence of God for Elimelech and his family.

> For to be carnally minded is death; but to be spiritually minded is life and peace. Because the carnal mind is enmity against God: for it is not subject to the law of God, neither indeed can be.
> —ROMANS 8:6–7

Allegorically, many believers find themselves living in an "idolatrous, foreign land" as a result of a famine of the presence of God in the personal lives of believers and in the church.

Q: *Examine your own spiritual life. Describe a time of famine when the presence of God was not evident in your life.*

Q: *What were the spiritual symptoms of famine that you experienced?*

> **Q:** *What were the circumstances that caused you to lose your song of joy?*

____

____

____

Causes of Spiritual Famine

How does famine come to the church? And perhaps more importantly, how can spiritual famine be averted?

Wrong government

Judges were ruling the land of Bethlehem-Judah when God withdrew His blessing, allowing famine to result. It was not in the divine order of God's plan of government to have judges rule the people. God had established a theocracy for his people and intended to rule as King Himself, speaking to His people through the prophets and priests.*

> In those days there was no king in Israel, but every man did that which was right in his own eyes.
>
> —JUDGES 17:6

> And he gave some, apostles; and some, prophets; and some, evangelists; and some, pastors and teachers; for the perfecting of the saints, for the work of the ministry, for the edifying of the body of Christ.
>
> —EPHESIANS 4:11–12

Q: What evidences of wrong government do you see in our world today?

Q: What evidences of wrong government exist within the church?

Q: What was God's intended pattern of government for the church (Eph. 4)?

Idolatry

The restoration of worship must be preceded by cleansing from idolatry. Our idols may not be made out of wood or stone and sitting in our houses, but they will be idols just the same—idols of our time, family, job, money, things, or friends.

Q: *Take a few minutes to examine your life and the life of your family. What "idols" may be evident in your family's life?*

____

____

Q: *How are they usurping the rightful place of God in your family life?*

____

____

Q: *Determine a specific course of action to eliminate these idols from your life. What will you do?*

____

____

Disobedience

Famine results when we continually transgress God's laws, knowing to do right and not doing it. Obedience to the laws of God brings wonderful blessings to our lives. The converse is also true—disobedience brings terrible consequences.*

> If ye be willing and obedient, ye shall eat the good of the land: But if ye shall refuse and rebel, ye shall be devoured with the sword: for the mouth of the Lord hath spoken it.
>
> —ISAIAH 1:19–20

Q: Are there any areas of disobedience in your life that may negate the blessings of God on your life? What are these areas of disobedience?

____

____

____

____

Lack of repentance

Revelation of the holiness of God brings revelation of our need for repentance. In the place of worship we are cleansed by the Holy Spirit.

> Then said I, Woe is me! for I am undone; because I am a man of unclean lips, and I dwell in the midst of a people of unclean lips; for mine eyes have seen the King, the LORD of hosts.
>
> —ISAIAH 6:5

Anything that keeps us out of the presence of God for any length of time will bring famine to our individual lives and churches.*

Q: *What may be keeping you out of the presence of God?*

Q: *Review the causes of famine listed in the preceding pages of this study guide. To which of the causes do you need to give priority attention?*

Q: *How will you eliminate this cause of famine from your life?*

Hope for the Church

After a long, dry, spiritual famine, God is beginning to visit the church in America with a renewal and refreshing that is crossing denominational barriers. This renewal is bringing repentance, release from offense, and is rekindling the prayer lives of many believers.*

Q: *How has God's fresh renewing brought an end to a time of famine in your own personal life?*

Q: *If you have not experienced a renewing and an end to famine in your own life, write a prayer asking God to bring such a renewal to your spiritual life. If you have been renewed, write a prayer of thanksgiving and gratitude to God.*

4

The Turning of Naomi

Decisions that require great changes in our lifestyles are never easy to make. Though Naomi may have longed many times to return to her homeland of Bethlehem-Judah where she was raised, she had undoubtedly grown accustomed to the life in Moab during the years she lived there. She had buried her loved ones in Moab and had become attached to her daughters-in-law as well. It would require a painful uprooting of her life once more in order to return to her homeland. Yet when she heard that God was visiting His people, her heart was stirred. It was this good news of God's visitation to His people that persuaded Naomi to return to the House of Bread.*

> Then she arose with her daughters in law, that she might return from the country of Moab: for she had heard in the country of Moab how that the LORD had visited his people in giving them

> bread. Wherefore she went forth out of the place where she was, and her two daughters in law with her; and they went on the way to return unto the land of Judah.
>
> —Ruth 1:6–7

Hunger: The Motivation for Return

Hunger for fresh bread can be a powerful motivating force in our spiritual lives. Hunger is:

- A state of need that refuses to be denied satisfaction.
- A gift of God.

Hunger was the motivation for the return of the prodigal son to his father's house.

> And when he came to himself, he said, How many hired servants of my father's have bread enough and to spare, and I perish with hunger! I will arise and go to my father.
>
> —Luke 15:17–18

A promise to satisfy the hunger of the believer is promised in the Beatitudes—the "constitution" of God's kingdom:

> Blessed are they which do hunger and thirst after righteousness: for they shall be filled.
>
> —Matthew 5:6

> **Q:** *Describe your own spiritual hunger.*

> **Q:** *How does God's promise to the believer to fill our hungry, empty spirits meet a specific point of hunger in your own life?*

In the Book of Ruth, Naomi declared her emptiness:

> I went out full, and the LORD hath brought me home again empty: why then call ye me Naomi, seeing the LORD hath testified against me, and the Almighty hath afflicted me?
>
> —RUTH 1:21

The Discipline of the Lord

Often we do not recognize the disciplining hand of God in our negative circumstances. We might not be so candid as Naomi to say that God has afflicted us, but we can relate to bitter experiences that brought us to God in our search for relief from our pain.

We must not consider painful times of chastening under the hand of God to be punishment. *Punishment* is "suffering, pain, or loss that serves as retribution." Christ bore the punishment for our sins on Calvary. There is a vast difference between discipline and punishment.*

God's discipline is correction with the motivation of shaping and molding us into His image. God's discipline is an important expression of God's love. It saves us from evil tendencies that would ultimately destroy us if left unchecked in our lives.

Q: *Think carefully about your own experiences with God's discipline. Describe the circumstances leading up to one time of being disciplined by God.*

____

____

Q: *What methods did God use to discipline you?*

____

____

Q: *How did this time of discipline express God's love to you?*

____

____

> **Q:** *What evil tendencies were you able to eliminate from your life as a result of this time of discipline?*

___

___

___

The purpose of God's discipline is to make disciples:

> For thus saith the high and lofty One that inhabiteth eternity, whose name is Holy; I dwell in the high and holy place, with him also that is of a contrite and humble spirit, to revive the spirit of the humble, and to revive the hearts of the contrite ones.
>
> —ISAIAH 57:15

Brokenness, which is often a result of discipline, is a prerequisite for truly finding God.* Brokenness is the first step to wholeness. Emptiness is the first step to being filled. The turning of hearts to God in deep contrition will bring revival to our lives.

His chastening, though painful, is always intended to bring redemption.*

The Barley Harvest

Naomi returned to Bethlehem-Judah at the *beginning of the barley harvest.* Barley was one of the most important grains raised in Palestine. It was grown chiefly for animal feed, but it was also eaten by the poor. It was sown in the fall and harvested in the spring.

Following the barley harvest, the first fruits were waved as an offering before the Lord (Lev. 3:12).

In the Old Testament, *offerings* were a foreshadowing of *worship* in the New Testament. *Wave offerings* foreshadowed the New Testament accounts of the *lifting of hands.*

Speaking allegorically, Naomi's return during the firstfruits of the barley harvest is being mirrored in the visitation of praise and worship the church has enjoyed during the last few years.*

Q: *How has your own praise and worship, or that of your church, changed as a result of your offering of the firstfruits of your life to God?*

____

____

____

Q: *How has your church learned to praise God in a new dimension as it turned its heart back to the House of Bread and opened its heart to the revival that is coming?*

____

____

____

> **Q:** *How would you like to see your own life or the life of your church changed in its expression of praise and worship?*

____

____

____

Harvest for the Poor

This harvest of praise and worship is for the poor:

> Blessed are the poor in spirit: for theirs is the kingdom of heaven.
>
> —MATTHEW 5:3

The first step in redemption is acknowledging our poverty of spirit. The barley harvest represents the beginning of redemption.

Naomi positioned herself for redemption by returning to the House of Bread. The church positions herself for complete restoration by choosing to respond to the news of God's fresh visitation among His people.

5

A Testing of Hearts

As is usually the case, Naomi's turning affected other lives besides her own. The lives of her daughters-in-law were intertwined with hers. They were faced with decisions regarding their own futures because of Naomi's decision to return to the House of Bread.... For Ruth and Orpah, going to the House of Bread meant leaving their homeland and kindred behind. It meant they would have to leave everything that was familiar to them, severing all family ties, to live as foreigners in the land of Bethlehem-Judah.*

As seen in Ruth 1:8–15, the *power of choice* is a key in personal restoration, as well as a key in possessing our inheritance in God. A testing of hearts is allowed by God to reveal our true motives.

Naomi's leaving Moab to return to Bethlehem-Judah tested the hearts of her daughters-in-law, Orpah and Naomi. Their choices revealed their character and ultimately determined their destinies.

Orpah

Orpah's name means "stiff-necked." It portrays an inflexible, unyielding character. Orpah chose to remain with the familiar. Because she did, she lost the touch of the presence of God she had seen in Naomi's life.

> Q: *Have you ever been stiff-necked in your response to God?*

____

____

> Q: *How have you demonstrated an inflexible, unyielding decision to remain with the familiar, refusing to move to a new spiritual place and thus losing the touch of the presence of God in your life?*

____

____

____

____

____

____

Ruth

Ruth means "friend." Her choice led her to her redemption. The key verse describing Ruth's choice is this:

> When she saw that she was *stedfastly minded to go with her,* then she left speaking unto her.
>
> —RUTH 1:18, EMPHASIS ADDED

Ruth's Sevenfold Declaration

Perhaps we cannot fully appreciate Ruth's idyllic love story until we analyze the treaty that eventually brought to her such good fortune. By treaty I do not mean a legal document, but the choices Ruth made before God. Those choices influenced her future as much as any legal treaty would have.*

1. "Whither thou goest, I will go" (1:16).
2. "Where thou lodgest, I will lodge" (1:16).
3. "Thy people shall be my people" (1:16).
4. "And thy God my God" (1:16).
5. "Where thou diest, will I die" (1:17).
6. "And there will I be buried" (1:17).
7. "The Lord do so to me, and more also, if aught but death part thee and me" (1:17).

Ruth is a literary classic, expressing extreme devotion, love, and loyalty. The secret of such love is kinship in the matters of the soul and of eternity. There can be no true love, no lasting loyalty, without this kinship of soul and spirit.*

Ruth's historical significance in the church is the inspiration to choose to live and die for God alone.

> **Q:** *Throughout the Book of Ruth, we are made aware of the power of our choices for blessing or for ill. How could your own future be altered if, by your choice, you pursued the godly principles revealed in Ruth's courageous treaty with Naomi?*

____

____

____

Ruth's "I Wills"

Contained within these seven declarations that Ruth made to Naomi are her "I wills." Each one expresses an aspect of her determined choice to follow Naomi to the House of Bread:

1.* "I will go"*—a faith decision

Though many people become attached to temporal things such as houses, lands, and personal relationships, the eternal reality is that home is wherever the will of God is for our lives. Other examples of this kind of faith decision are given in the Word of God:

- *David*—Psalm 71:16
- *Elisha*—2 Kings 6:3
- *Samson*—Judges 16:20
- *Deborah*—Judges 4:9
- *Rebekah*—Genesis 24:58
- *The prodigal son*—Luke 15:18

Faith decisions underscore the power of choice to affect our lives for good or ill.

> **Q:** *Look up each Scripture reference given above, and beside each person's name in the list below, describe the details of that person's "I will" faith decision.*

David ______________________________

Elisha ______________________________

Samson ______________________________

Deborah ______________________________

Rebekah ______________________________

The prodigal son ______________________________

> **Q:** *Now describe from your own life experiences a time when you made a determined "I will" faith decision to obey God in a specific circumstance.*

____

____

____

2. "I will lodge"—*a permanent decision*

Ruth's choice to renounce her homeland and cut all human ties to her own people required profound commitment.

> **Q:** *Such a decision is no small matter even today in our mobile culture. Describe a time when you made a permanent, profound commitment to renounce something for the Lord.*

---

3. "Thy people shall be my people"—*identification decision*

To fellowship with God, one must fellowship and unite with the people of God. What lovely surprises were in store for Ruth based on this decision! Ruth never had cause to regret her decision.

4. "Thy God shall be my God"—*a fixed decision*

Ruth's heart was fixed; her mind was made up. Her earthly and worldly associations were sacrificed.

> **Q:** *What "lovely surprises" have come your way as a result of your decision to sacrifice earthly, worldly associations to serve only God?*

---

5. "Where thou diest, will I die"*—eternal decision*

Ruth was steadfast. She had settled the question of how she would live and where she would die. She had no regrets or fickleness in her resolve to follow God all the way.

6. "And there will I be buried"*—final decision*

Even in burial, there was to be no hearkening back to the land of Moab. Her grave would be sealed among the people of God with whom she lived.

7. "The Lord do so to me, and more also, if aught but death part me and thee"*—irrevocable decision*

As a final sign of her determination to make the choice to follow Naomi, Ruth sealed her decision with a covenant, made in the strength of the Lord and His name and before His face. The Scripture tells us that "Ruth clave unto her [Naomi]" (Ruth 1:14).

> Q: *Have you been required to make such an irrevocable and permanent decision to serve Christ?*

____

____

____

____

____

Q: *Describe this decision.*

Q: *What have been the costs of this decision?*

Q: *What have been the blessings?*

Obedience Precedes Revelation

As we choose to obey His will, we receive a greater revelation of truth. God's divine will is executed when we choose His will and die to ours. The psalmist gives us a wonderful understanding of the "I wills" of God for the person who exchanges his own will for God's wonderful promises:

> Because he hath set his love upon me, therefore will I deliver him: I will set him on high, because he hath known my name. He shall call upon me, and I will answer him: I will be with him in trouble; I will deliver him, and honor him. With long life will I satisfy him, and show him my salvation.
>
> —Psalm 91:14–16

The end of commitment is a love relationship with Jesus. This relationship comes out of complete surrender to Him. God and His will for our lives are the only things that will satisfy our hearts.

Ruth's Commitment

In Ruth 1:16–17 we see Ruth's commitment to Naomi and Naomi's God, and we recognize the cry of the church for intimate relationship with the living God.

In order to enter into this love relationship with Jesus, the church must do the following things, as depicted in Ruth 1:19–22.

- Decide to return to the place of God's presence (worship).

- Turn from the idolatry of worldly culture and embrace the "promised land" of God's kingdom.
- Cut all ties to the carnal way of life that surrounds her.
- Abandon herself in utter trust to the living God.

What is the key to the redemption of Naomi and Ruth? In the time of testing they made a complete commitment to serve the living God.

> **Q:** *Write a prayer expressing to God your complete commitment to serve Him in spite of the times of testing you may be facing.*

____

____

____

____

____

____

Poor in Spirit

Naomi was emotionally broken ("call me Mara [bitter]") and humbled through poverty. Whatever her emotional state, the important thing was that Naomi was home where God could continue His redemption in her life.*

Such a wonderful love story can be ours as well if we choose to come into relationship with our Kinsman-Redeemer, serving Him with a heart filled with humble gratitude and love. The constitution of the kingdom—the Beatitudes—declares:

> Blessed are the poor in spirit: for theirs is the kingdom of heaven.
>
> —Matthew 5:3

Being "poor in spirit" means we are humble enough to acknowledge our need of God. In that acknowledgment, God will provide for us what we need to fulfill His purposes for us.*

6

Tenderness Toward the Helpless

The Law of Moses, given to the children of Israel by God, made provision for the redemption of the poor.

> And Naomi had a kinsman of her husband's, a mighty man of wealth, of the family of Elimelech; and his name was Boaz. And Ruth the Moabitess said unto Naomi, Let me now go to the field, and glean ears of corn after him in whose sight I shall find grace. And she said unto her, Go, my daughter.
>
> —Ruth 2:1–2

Redemption of the Poor

The Law of Moses stated that if someone became so poor that he could not pay his debts, he could sell his land and/or himself to pay his debtors (Lev. 25:47–54). There were three manners of redemption:

1. If the individual could accumulate enough to buy back the land, he was free to do so (Lev. 25:26–27, 49–50).

2. If he could not buy back his land, he would have to work as a hired hand until the Year of Jubilee—celebrated every fifty years—when the land went back to the original owner and debtor-slaves were set free (Lev. 25:28, 54).

3. If one of his blood relatives had the means to pay the price of redemption, that relative would purchase what his indebted relative had sold (Lev. 25:25, 47–53).

The Law of Moses made provision for widows (Deut. 25:5–10):

1. A widow's son(s) was given the responsibility for her care.

2. If a widow had no son, the brother of her husband was responsible to marry her and raise up seed for his brother's house.

The Book of Ruth outlines Naomi's plight: She was destitute and without husband or sons to care for her. Though her plight seemed desperate, Naomi knew there was a means of redemption provided for her according to the Law of Moses. In type, these laws foreshadow the wonderful, eternal redemption that Christ has provided for mankind.*

Beyond the Cross: A Relationship of Choice

Sacrifice of Christ	On Calvary Christ redeemed man from the curse of sin with His blood.
Eternal Salvation	Is accepting the sacrifice of Christ for our sins.
Maturity	Our choice of living in obedience to Christ; being transformed into His image; entering into a love relationship with Him; allowing the character of God to be formed in us.

Q: The maturity that reflects Christ's character in our lives comes only as we choose to live in obedience to Him. How have you chosen to be obedient to Christ?

Q: What evidence does your life show of transformation into His image?

Q: *Describe the intimacy of your relationship with Christ.*

____

____

____

____

Q: *What evidence can you demonstrate to show that His character is being formed in you?*

____

____

____

____

> Until we all attain to the unity of the faith, and of the knowledge of the Son of God, to a mature man, to the measure of the stature which belongs to the fulness of Christ.
>
> —EPHESIANS 4:13, NAS

Our relationship of love and obedience to God brings us to maturity in our Christian character and qualifies us to become part of the bride of Christ.*

The key to complete restoration is our choice to forsake all to belong to Christ.

Covenant Promises

The provision for Naomi's and Ruth's redemption was made through the Law of Moses centuries before their births. The provision for our redemption was made before the foundation of the world:

> . . . the Lamb slain from the foundation of the world.
>
> —REVELATION 13:8

God's Sovereign Intervention

God can, and does, intervene in our lives sovereignly. We could not come to Him except He draws us (John 6:44).

> We love him, because he first loved us.
>
> —1 JOHN 4:19

God initiates His work of grace in our lives…we must acknowledge our need of Him in order to find Him.*

Our deep inner sense of need causes us to cry out to God. And God promises us:

> Blessed are the poor in spirit: for theirs is the kingdom of heaven.
>
> —MATTHEW 5:3

When Jesus declared those words, He was referring to that deep inner sense of need that causes us to cry out to God. When we do that, we will find the whole kingdom of heaven at our disposal.*

Q: Has a deep inner sense of need caused you to cry out to God?

Q: Describe your cry and God's response to you.

7

Prevenient Grace

P*revenient grace* is the sovereign working of God to direct a life that has been surrendered to Him.

> And she went, and came, and gleaned in the field after the reapers: and her hap was to light on a part of the field belonging unto Boaz, who was of the kindred of Elimelech.
>
> —RUTH 2:3

God's prevenient grace operates in the circumstances of our lives beyond our knowledge and takes care of us even when we don't know what is happening in the unseen world. That sovereign eye of God guided Ruth to the field of Boaz, her kinsman-redeemer.*

The Redeemer

The English word *kinsman* has three Hebrew words

that correspond. The first two, *modo* and *qarob,* define "a near relative linked to one by family ties." The third word, *goel,* carries the connotation of "kinsman-redeemer." The kinsman-redeemer was "one who has the right to redeem." He was:

- A *near kinsman.*
- One who had the *power* to redeem (financial means).
- One who was *willing* to redeem (willing to pay the price).
- The only one who had the *right to buy back* property sold to another.

It was a lifelong responsibility. *Redemption requires continued relationship between the redeemer and the redeemed.*

Jesus—our heavenly Goel

Jesus met all of the above requirements to allow Him to be the Kinsman-Redeemer of all mankind:

- He held the relationship of Son to Father God, yet He humbled Himself to be a man to be in relationship to us.
- He led a sinless life in perfect obedience to the Father to become the spotless Lamb that satisfied the judgment for mankind's sin.
- He was willing to pay the price—that of crucifixion.
- He is the only One worthy to redeem mankind.

And they sung a new song, saying, Thou are

> worthy to take the book, and to open the seals thereof: for thou wast slain, and hast redeemed us to God by thy blood out of every kindred, and tongue, and people, and nation.
>
> —REVELATION 5:9

Our highest worship of Jesus is as the slain Lamb, our Kinsman-Redeemer.

> Looking unto Jesus the author and finisher of our faith; who for the joy that was set before him endured the cross, despising the shame, and is set down at the right hand of the throne of God.
>
> —HEBREWS 12:2

A *goel* redeems by choosing to become responsible for another's life.

> I am the good shepherd: the good shepherd giveth his life for the sheep. . . . As the Father knoweth me, even so know I the Father: and I lay down my life for the sheep.
>
> —JOHN 10:11, 15

Jesus' redemptive work was more than a blotting out of our sins; complete redemption denotes a continuing love relationship with our Redeemer. We must not underestimate the value of the sacrifice Jesus made in order to become our Kinsman-Redeemer.

> Forasmuch as ye know that ye were not redeemed with corruptible things, as silver and gold, from your vain conversation received by

> tradition from your fathers; but with the precious blood of Christ, as of a lamb without blemish and without spot.
>
> —1 PETER 1:18–19

Q: *Describe the sacrifice that Jesus—your Kinsman-Redeemer—made in order to buy back your redemption.*

Q: *To whom (or what) had you become enslaved?*

Q: *How have you, or will you, strive to develop a continuing love relationship with your Redeemer?*

> **Q:** *How has He continued to show His love for you?*

____

____

____

Tender Watchings: Boaz As a Type of Christ

Ruth found herself in the field of Boaz, her kinsman-redeemer, though she did not know it at the time. She was aware only of her hunger and of the provision of the Law that allowed her to glean in the land where there was a great harvest.* (See Ruth 2:4–12.)

As Christians, we can expect approval and personal attention such as Boaz gave to Ruth from Jesus, our heavenly Boaz, when we seek to satisfy our hunger in His "field." In this we will find revelation of Jesus in His Word.

> It is written, Man shall not live by bread alone, but by every word that proceedeth out of the mouth of God.
>
> —MATTHEW 4:4

> I am the way, the truth, and the life.
>
> —JOHN 14:6

> I am Alpha and Omega.
>
> —REVELATION 1:8

At a time of desperation, loss, and hunger, Ruth

sought only to live within the confines of the Law. Yet her kinsman-redeemer appeared and redeemed her above the limitations of the Law to satisfy her hunger and bless her life with an intimate relationship of love with her kinsman-redeemer.

Q: *How has Christ, your Kinsman-Redeemer, entered your life at a time of desperation, loss, and hunger to raise you above the restrictions of the Law to a life of intimate relationship with Him?*

8

The Treatment of Ruth

In verses 8–9 and 13–16 of Ruth 2, Boaz exceeded the usual attitude of tolerance toward gleaners in his culture. He commended Ruth for her care of her mother-in-law and invited her to stay in his fields, offering her the privilege of drinking the water his servants had brought. He commanded them to respect her and protect her from harm.*

The Process of Redemption

Boaz's treatment of Ruth reflects the loving heart of Jesus our Redeemer. Boaz was impressed by Ruth's character, choices, and consistency. Allegorically, we glimpse the loving heart of our great Redeemer through Boaz. Jesus values and responds to our desire for and devotion to Him. We find grace in His eyes as we continually come to "glean" truth and life from Him for ourselves and for others in need.*

Provision of water

> . . . and when thou art athirst, go unto the vessels, and drink of that which the young men have drawn.
>
> —RUTH 2:9

Allegorically, this provision of water is very significant. Jesus offered water to the woman at the well in John 4. He told the Samaritan woman that His living water would satisfy her thirst and spring up inside like a well.

> ...a well of water springing up into everlasting life.
>
> —JOHN 4:14

Throughout the Scriptures, saints can be tracked by following their altars and wells. . . . The church needs to be a place where altars of commitment and worship are built and wells of water are dug in our own lives to sustain us and provide life for others. . . . Our lives must be continually surrendered to the Holy Spirit and filled with His life-giving presence as we live in daily prayer and the Word of God.*

> *Q: How has Christ fulfilled your thirst?*

____

____

____

Q: *Look outside your own personal experience of thirst to the thirst you see evident in the life of someone you know or love. Describe the circumstances that have brought thirst to that person.*

Q: *How could the living water freely offered from Christ, their Kinsman-Redeemer, satisfy their thirst as He has satisfied yours?*

Q: *Write a prayer asking Christ to prepare you to be the one who can introduce that person to the living water from Christ.*

The Promise of Protection

Boaz commanded his servants not to insult or make improper advances toward Ruth nor to reproach or rebuke her. This promise of protection released Ruth from fear of harm and gave her peace of mind as she gleaned among the men in the field.*

> Let thine eyes be on the field that they do reap, and go thou after them: have I not charged the young men that they shall not touch thee?
>
> —RUTH 2:9

As Boaz promised Ruth protection while gleaning in his fields, the church should provide a safe place for those who come to "glean." The church should be a safe place where people can come to find solace and comfort from the evils of the world.

> Let nothing be done through strife or vainglory; but in lowliness of mind let each esteem other better than themselves. Look not every man on his own things, but every man also on the things of others.
>
> —PHILIPPIANS 2:3–4

> **Q:** *Describe the ways in which your church offers a safe haven to people from the evils of the world.*

> **Q:** *How could your church improve upon its care and protection of others?*

Handfuls on Purpose

Boaz invited Ruth to sit beside the reapers at meal time and eat the bread provided for them. He gave her parched corn as she sat at the table with him. He also told his servants to allow her to glean among the sheaves and to drop handfuls of barley on purpose for her.

> And Boaz said unto her, At mealtime come thou hither, and eat of the bread, and dip thy morsel in the vinegar. And she sat beside the reapers: and he reached her parched corn, and she did eat, and was sufficed, and left. And

> when she was risen up to go glean, Boaz commanded his young men, saying, Let her glean even among the sheaves, and reproach her not: And let fall also some of the handfuls on purpose for her, and leave them, that she may glean them, and rebuke her not.
>
> —RUTH 2:14–16

Boaz demonstrated his personal interest in Ruth through his personal attention and preferential treatment of her.

How did Ruth gain this place of favor? She did it by her humility, her faithful attachment to her mother-in-law, and her love to the God of Israel.*

Our Redeemer desires to give us handfuls of revelation as we sit in His presence and feed on His Word. He loves to give us handfuls of revelation that feed and strengthen our souls. He gives us an abundant supply to take to others.

Q: *How has Christ demonstrated His personal interest in you by giving you "handfuls of revelation" that were exactly what you needed for a specific situation or circumstance?*

____

____

____

____

> *Q: How has He enabled you to provide such revelation to someone else who needed fresh revelation upon the situations or circumstances of their life?*

____

____

____

____

Provision shared

At the end of the day, Ruth hurried home to Naomi with her arms full of grain and her heart full of gratitude and joy.

> So she gleaned in the field until even, and beat out that she had gleaned: and it was about an ephah of barley. And she took it up, and went into the city: and her mother in law saw what she had gleaned: and she brought forth, and gave to her that she had reserved after she was sufficed.
>
> —RUTH 2:17–18

The Levirate Law

The significance of Boaz's role is heightened as we understand the levirate law that was followed in Israel during that time. The root word of *levirate* is *levir,* which actually means "husband's brother" (brother-in-law). (See Deuteronomy 25:5–10.)

This law stated that the surviving brother of a

deceased man could marry his brother's widow; the children of this union would be as the offspring and heirs of his dead brother. The law also allowed the *levir* the option of refusal.

Boaz was not the nearest kinsman to Naomi and Ruth; he was not obligated by the levirate law to redeem them. Boaz operated under a higher law—the law of love.

Allegorically, it follows that we have been eternally blessed because God became our friend, our hero, our Redeemer, though we were foreigners to His kingdom. Christ proved His friendship to us, being willing to do all we need for our redemption. He lived and died to show us this higher law of grace revealed through love.*

The name *Boaz* means "in him is strength." Christ had the strength to accomplish the purposes of God for all mankind. Boaz was characterized by grace.

> And, behold, Boaz came from Bethlehem, and said unto the reapers, The Lord be with you. And they answered him, The Lord bless thee.
>
> —Ruth 2:4

Grace is not merely a theological term that describes the New Covenant superseding the Law of Moses. *Grace* is the "wonderful redemptive response of love that is not required by law." It is when one stoops from his position to extend comfort and help to one who is not worthy. This higher law of grace was working in Boaz, foreshadowing the love of our Savior that caused Him to sacrifice His life to redeem mankind.*

Grace to Redeem

Because of the grace working in Boaz, though he was not strictly bound by the levirate law, he chose to redeem Ruth.*

> And her mother in law said unto her, Where hast thou gleaned to day? and where wroughtest thou? blessed be he that did take knowledge of thee. And she shewed her mother in law with whom she had wrought, and said, The man's name with whom I wrought to day is Boaz. And Naomi said unto her daughter in law, Blessed be he of the LORD, who hath not left off his kindness to the living and to the dead. And Naomi said unto her, The man is near of kin unto us, one of our next kinsmen.
>
> —RUTH 2:19–20

The word *kin* (Hebrew, *qarob*) is used to mean "a relative." The word *kinsman* is a completely different word. Kinsman is the word *goel* in Hebrew, defined as "one who has the right to redeem."

Jesus made Himself our "near kinsman" in order to become our Kinsman-Redeemer:

> But made himself of no reputation, and took upon him the form of a servant, and was made in the likeness of men: And being found in fashion as a man, he humbled himself, and became obedient into death, even the death of the cross.
>
> —PHILIPPIANS 2:7–8

The church is redeemed from "widowhood" as Christians. The church will come into a greater relationship with her Redeemer than she has ever known. Our Kinsman-Redeemer has provided us with the benefits of our redemption:

1. Our return to the House of Bread (place of worship and relationship with Jesus).

2. The opportunity to glean in the field of our Kinsman-Redeemer (seek revelation in the Word).

3. The privilege of enjoying His provision and safety (become a part of His church).

4. The right to dine in His presence (come into personal fellowship with Jesus).

Think about your personal experience of redemption. Answer each of the following questions specifically, describing your redemption.

Q: *How has redemption returned you to a place of worship and relationship with Jesus?*

____

____

____

> **Q:** *How can you demonstrate your opportunities to see revelation in the Word?*

___

___

___

> **Q:** *What has become your place of ministry and discipleship as a part of His church?*

___

___

___

> **Q:** *Describe your times of personal fellowship with Christ.*

___

___

___

Fullness of Time

The four benefits listed above are the precursors to complete restoration. Naomi seemed to be awating the opportune time to reveal the full plan for Ruth's redemption by Boaz.

> And Ruth the Moabitess said, He said unto me also, Thou shalt keep fast by my young men, until they have ended all my harvest. And Naomi said unto Ruth her daughter in law, It is good, my daughter, that thou go out with his maidens, that they meet thee not in any other field. So she kept fast by the maidens of Boaz to glean unto the end of barley harvest and of wheat harvest; and dwelt with her mother in law.
>
> —RUTH 2:21–23

The Scriptures reveal that there is always a time element involved in redemption, an "opportune time." By her obedience, Ruth was allowed to reap the rewards of obedience (verse 23).

> Q: *Do you have a sense that your redemption has not been fully completed yet?*

> Q: *What are the "unknowns" about your spiritual experience? What areas of your life still need to be transformed by full redemption?*

Q: Write a prayer commiting your obedience to your Kinsman-Redeemer and asking Him to complete the act of redemption in your life.

9

Tarrying for the Appointment

Obedience is the prerequisite for finding rest. Ruth had worked diligently for many weeks, gleaning throughout both the barley and the wheat harvests in the field of Boaz. The harvesters were busy at the threshing floor, taking advantage of the cool evening breezes to winnow their grain. Naomi knew that Boaz could be found on the threshing floor, winnowing the harvested grain until late at night.*

Best of Relationships

> Then Naomi her mother in law said unto her, My daughter, shall I not seek rest for thee, that it may be well with thee?
>
> —RUTH 3:1

What was this rest that Naomi desired for Ruth? It is clear from the context that the rest Naomi was referring to was not merely physical rest. Rather she spoke of a wonderful state of grace that Ruth had not yet known, a rest of relationship that she had not yet entered into.*

> There remaineth therefore a rest to the people of God.
>
> —HEBREWS 4:9

The state of *rest* that is available to the believer through a relationship with Christ, our Kinsman-Redeemer:

- Is a state of grace.
- Is entered by faith.
- Involves intimate relationship with Christ.
- Provides a life filled with security and freedom.

> Behold, I stand at the door, and knock: if any man hear my voice, and open the door, I will come in to him, and will sup with him, and he with me.
>
> —REVELATION 3:20

The word *sup* is used only three times in Scripture, and it means "communion." True communion involves a spiritual relationship of intimate love with our Redeemer. It is a place of complete surrender to the Bridegroom. In that relationship, Christ gives divine revelation, impregnating the spirit of His bride with the living Word.*

> **Q:** *Have you reached the place of rest in your relationship with Christ?*

___

___

> **Q:** *In your relationship with Christ, how has He impregnated your spirit with His living Word?*

___

___

___

___

As it did for Ruth, this rest provides:

- A secure future.
- The removal of the reproach of widowhood.
- Freedom from poverty and the right to prosperity and honor.

> For thus saith the Lord GOD, the Holy One of Israel; In returning and rest shall ye be saved; in quietness and in confidence shall be your strength.
>
> —ISAIAH 30:15

Instructions for Entering Into True Revelation of Our Bridegroom-Redeemer

In Ruth 3:2–6, Naomi shared with Ruth her plan to

seek redemption through Boaz, their near kinsman.

As we apply the allegorical truths that Naomi's instructions reveal to our Christian walk, we will learn what is involved in entering into true revelation of our Bridegroom-Redeemer.*

1. Wash thyself—cleansing from all that pollutes our soul

We are cleansed from sin by the blood of Christ. We are sanctified by the *washing of water by the Word.*

> Husbands, love your wives, even as Christ also loved the church, and gave himself for it; that he might sanctify and cleanse it with the washing of water by the word, that he might present it to himself a glorious church, not having spot, or wrinkle, or any such thing; but that it should be holy and without blemish.
>
> —EPHESIANS 5:25–27

> Sanctify them through thy truth: thy word is truth.
>
> —JOHN 17:17

> Q: *How have you washed yourself by His Word, cleansing your life from all that would pollute your soul?*

____

____

____

2. Anoint thyself—continual anointing of believers

It is important to realize that believers are anointed not just once, but continually as we allow the Holy Spirit to fill us with the divine fragrance of Christ. Anointing destroys the yoke of bondage.

> . . . and the yoke shall be destroyed because of the anointing.
>
> —ISAIAH 10:27

The Holy Spirit's anointing cleanses us from the "filthiness of the flesh."

> Having therefore these promises, dearly beloved, let us cleanse ourselves from all filthiness of the flesh and spirit, perfecting holiness in the fear of God.
>
> —2 CORINTHIANS 7:1

The anointing allows others to sense the presence of God in our lives through our actions and reactions. It is our preparation for meeting our Redeemer.

> Thou lovest righteousness, and hatest wickedness: therefore God, thy God, hath anointed thee with the oil of gladness above thy fellows.
>
> —PSALM 45:7

> **Q:** *Describe a time when you felt the anointing of God upon your life.*

___

___

___

3. Put on your raiment—garment of praise; the "new man" in Christ

> To appoint unto them that mourn in Zion, to give unto them beauty for ashes, the oil of joy for mourning, the garment of praise for the spirit of heaviness.
>
> —Isaiah 61:3

> By him therefore let us offer the sacrifice of praise to God continually, that is, the fruit of our lips giving thanks to his name.
>
> —Hebrews 13:15

> Set your affection of things above, not on things on the earth. . . . Mortify therefore your members which are upon the earth. . . . Lie not to one another, seeing that you have put off the old man with his deeds; and have put on the new man, which is renewed in knowledge after the image of him that created him.
>
> —Colossians 3:2, 5, 9–10

Brides don't wear mourning garments. They are dressed in once-in-a-lifetime elegance in anticipation of the happy event that is about to take place. It was in anticipation of Ruth's redemption that Naomi instructed Ruth to put off her widow's garment and put on her best raiment.*

> **Q:** *What evidence in your life points to the removal of the "garments of mourning" and the addition of the "garment of praise" in your spiritual experience?*

___

___

___

4. Go to the threshing floor—endure God's cleansing works

The festivity and joy of harvest that Ruth experienced are a foreshadowing of the reality of *praise and worship* in the church today. The allegorical picture of the winnowing and threshing at the time of harvest depicts the cleansing work of the Holy Spirit in the life of the believer.

> He [Jesus] shall baptize you with the Holy Ghost, and with fire: Whose fan is in his hand, and he will throughly purge his floor, and gather his wheat into the garner; but he will burn up the chaff with unquenchable fire.
>
> —MATTHEW 3:11–12

Believers should expect to endure a threshing-floor experience when the Lord Himself comes to separate the wheat from the chaff in our lives. Obedience is always a result of faith, of believing the promises of God to the extent that we act on them.*

> **Q:** *Has God required a time of winnowing and threshing in your spiritual life since Christ redeemed you from your poverty and loss? Describe this experience.*

____

____

____

5. Stand in the shadows—wait upon the Lord

The requirement of waiting is a part of our redemption. Ruth lay at Boaz's feet and waited to see what he would do for her. Jesus waited in prayer. Jesus commended Mary of Bethany for sitting at His feet. We become worshipers by waiting.

Whom we become in our relationship with Christ will be the result of our choice to wait on Him.*

> **Q:** *Has the Lord required a time of waiting in your life? Describe your feelings as you wait upon the Lord.*

____

____

____

Boaz's Response

Ruth 3:7–13 tells us that Ruth went in to where Boaz was sleeping. That night when Boaz detected a woman lying at his feet in the dark, he did not ask her what she wanted—he understood what she wanted. Rather his question to her was, "Who art thou?" In simply saying her name, Ruth revealed the need of her life.*

Spreading garment: protection

In Eastern culture, to spread a skirt, or covering, over someone was a symbolic act offering that person protection. More than that, it involved entering into covenant with a person for the sake of redemption.*

> Now when I passed by thee, and looked upon thee, behold, thy time was the time of love; and I spread my skirt over thee, and covered thy nakedness: yea, I swear unto thee, and entered into a covenant with thee, saith the Lord GOD, and thou becamest mine.
>
> —EZEKIEL 16:8

Ruth typifies the helpless state of every person to redeem themselves. The key to our redemption is acknowledging our helpless state and our need for redemption. When Christians wait in the presence of their Redeemer, aware of their need of His redeeming power, they will receive revelation of their true nature in the light of His holiness. That carnal nature that wages war against our spirits will be exposed in the presence of God.*

> But we all, with open face beholding as in a glass the glory of the Lord, are changed into the same image from glory to glory, even as by the Spirit of the Lord.
>
> —2 CORINTHIANS 3:18

Process of Growth to Maturity

There are two important steps in our process of growth toward maturity:

1. Waiting in His presence.
2. Confessing who we are in light of who He is.

> **Q:** *With which of these two steps are you having the greatest struggle? Describe your struggle.*

____

____

____

____

____

Ruth 3:14–18 tells us that once again Ruth was required to wait. There is a place of restful hope for us that we can find only after we have asked our Redeemer to "spread His skirt over us."

10

Trial of the Kinsman

Only the matter of the nearer kinsman that must yet be resolved stood in the way of Ruth's wonderful restoration. As we understand whom this kinsman foreshadows, we will understand the difficulty we encounter in securing our own redemption even after we have submitted ourselves to our lovely Redeemer. We too have a nearer kinsman that must be confronted before we can enjoy complete restoration.*

Sitting at the Gates

Ruth 4:1 states that Boaz sat at the city gates. His place among the elders at the city gates indicated his:

- Moral character
- Wealth
- Social rank

The city gates served as the seat of justice:

> Enter into his gates with thanksgiving, and into his courts with praise: be thankful unto him, and bless his name.
>
> —PSALM 100:4

The gates of the city of God denote coming to the seat of divine justice.

Boaz's Mission

Boaz was ready to challenge the nearer kinsman for the redemption of Elimelech's inheritance, which included Ruth the Moabitess. The steps of this encounter included:

1. Meeting with the ten elders of the city to present his proposition (Ruth 4:2).
2. Proposing to the nearer kinsman his legal requirement to buy the inheritance of Elimelech (4:3–4).
3. The nearer kinsman consenting to redeem the inheritance at first (4:4).
4. Boaz then declaring that the redemption of Ruth was a part of the proposition (4:5).
5. The nearer kinsman refusing to redeem Ruth for fear of marring his own inheritance. He was not willing to marry this foreigner and ruin his bloodline for the sake of his posterity (4:6).

The Nearer Kinsman

Whom does this nearer kinsman represent allegorically? Three different explanations of his role have been given:

1. Some Bible scholars feel he is a type of the world system: the many-faceted force that drives people to succeed.

2. Others believe him to be a type of the Law of Moses, given before Calvary and powerless to redeem.

> Wherefore the law was our schoolmaster to bring us unto Christ, that we might be justified by faith.
>
> —GALATIANS 3:24

3. A third view presents him as a type of every person's carnal nature or self-life.

> So then with the mind I myself serve the law of God; but with the flesh the law of sin.
>
> —ROMANS 7:25

> And that ye put on the new man, which after God is created in righteousness and true holiness.
>
> —EPHESIANS 4:24

Whether we conclude that, in type, Ruth's nearer kinsman foreshadows the world system, the Law of Moses, or our carnal nature, it is clear that he stands for everything that says *no* to God's redemptive will for our lives.

> ***Q:*** *As you consider your own personal struggle to mature spiritually, have you struggled with any of these three nearer kinsmen?*

____

____

> ***Q:*** *Describe your struggle with each.*

The world system and the struggle to succeed: ____________

____.

The Law and your incapability to keep it: ____________

____.

Your carnal nature or self-life: ____________

____.

> ***Q:*** *With which of these three do you still struggle the most?*

____

____

____

Through His obedience, Jesus challenged the right of the "nearer kinsman" to redeem us, fulfilling the Law of Moses through a sinless life. Jesus' redemption of mankind is a reordering of authority for Law, grace, and the flesh; the Law yielded to grace in the blood atonement, and the flesh was crucified. Both the Law and the sin-nature (sinful self-life) were dealt with on Calvary.

> I am the good shepherd: the good shepherd giveth his life for the sheep.... No man taketh it from me, but I lay it down myself. I have power to lay it down, and I have power to take it again. This commandment have I received of my Father.
>
> —JOHN 10:11, 18

Sealing the covenant

> Now this was the manner in former time in Israel concerning redeeming and concerning changing, for to confirm all things; a man plucked off his shoe, and gave it to his neighbour: and this was a testimony in Israel. Therefore the kinsman said unto Boaz, Buy it for thee. So he drew off his shoe.
>
> —RUTH 4:7–8

This ancient custom originated with the ancient practice of taking possession of fixed property by treading the soil:

> Every place that the sole of your foot shall tread upon, that have I given unto you, as I said unto Moses.
>
> —JOSHUA 1:3

In later times, this act of taking off one's shoe and handing it to the person to whom property was being transferred was a sign of the sealing of a covenant. It is a symbol of transfer of possession or right of ownership. Allegorically, it is a picture of the eternal redemption of Christ:

> And I will put enmity between thee and the woman, and between thy seed and her seed; it shall bruise thy head, and thou shalt bruise his heel.
>
> —GENESIS 3:15

> For this purpose the Son of God was manifested, that he might destroy the works of the devil.
>
> —1 JOHN 3:8

The word *destroy* here means "to undo, outdo, and overdo" everything the devil ever did. Jesus will undo for us everything that needs to be undone so that we can fulfill our divine destiny in God.

> **Q:** *What works of the devil has God undone in your life, freeing you to the divine destiny for your life?*

____

____

____

____

Witnesses to the Deed

Just as the elders were witnesses to Boaz's deed in Ruth 4:9–12, the church stands as witness today that Christ has sealed the covenant of our redemption in His blood:

> Neither by the blood of goats and calves, but by his own blood he entered in once into the holy place, having obtained eternal redemption for us.
>
> —Hebrews 9:12

The power of the Holy Spirit enables us to choose God's will.*

> If any man will come after me, let him deny himself, and take up his cross daily, and follow me.
>
> —Luke 9:23

> I die daily.
>
> —1 Corinthians 15:31

11

Triumph and Transformation

The wonder of redemption is that it restores us to a place of greater blessing than we enjoyed before our unfortunate loss. When Christ our Kinsman-Redeemer comes to buy back everything we have lost, the quality of divine life He gives us thrusts us into a greater dimension of eternal worth than we have ever known.*

Eternal Significance

We can see the principle of eternal significance at work in the lives of Naomi and Ruth. Ruth 4:13–22 shows how they became a part of the genealogy of Jesus. Through Jesus, our heavenly Boaz and Kinsman-Redeemer, we also have become a part of the bloodline of Christ.

Naomi and Ruth	Entered into the genealogy of Jesus.
Obed	The son of Boaz and Ruth; his name means "the serving one." He foreshadows the life of Christ being reproduced in the church.
Ephratah	The people prayed for Ruth to "do thou worthily in Ephratah and be famous in Bethlehem" (Ruth 4:11). *Ephratah* means "fruitful." It foreshadows the calling of the church to beget and train worthy sons and daughters.
Jesse	The son of Obed.
David	The son of Jesse.

Christ's work of redemption brings us to divine rest, forms His character in us, and causes us to bring forth fruit in His kingdom (sons and daughters who love God).

> Q: *Give an illustration of how God is causing you to bring forth fruit in His kingdom.*

____

____

____

____

____

____

An Eternal Kingdom

Like the nation of Israel, the church has endured multiple persecutions and times of bondage, and yet both survive while ungodly kingdoms and the philosophies of men have come and gone.

Like Ruth, the church will be restored through revival of relationship with her Kinsman-Redeemer. The keys to this redemption and restoration are:

- Faith
- Humility
- Obedience

The posture of the church is to wait for the promise of redemption:

> Now unto him that is able to keep you from falling, and to present you faultless before the presence of his glory with exceeding joy, to the only wise God our Savior, be glory and majesty, dominion and power, both now and ever. Amen.
>
> —JUDE 24–25

12

This Present Light

Have we grasped the magnitude and wonder of God's plan for restoration for our individual lives and for His church as it is foreshadowed prophetically in the Book of Ruth? Or do our minds defeat us as we think, *It's too good to be true; maybe someday, but surely not now*. Can we really hope to be a part of a church "without spot or wrinkle" in our day?

> Arise, shine; for thy light is come, and the glory of the LORD is risen upon thee. For, behold, the darkness shall cover the earth, and gross darkness the people: but the LORD shall arise upon thee, and his glory shall be seen upon thee.
>
> —ISAIAH 60:1–2

"I AM"—Present Reality of Christ As Our Kinsman-Redeemer

Christ does not relate to mankind in the past tense or

in the future tense. He does not acknowledge our time limitations of past or future. Let's take a look at who Christ is in the reality of our lives today.

- "Before Abraham was, I am" (John 8:58).
- "I am the way, the truth, and the life: no man cometh to the Father, but by me" (John 14:6).
- "I am the living bread which came down from heaven: if any man eat of this bread, he shall live forever" (John 6:51).
- "I am the resurrection and the life" (John 11:25).
- "I am the door" (John 10:9).
- "I am the good shepherd" (John 10:11).
- "I am the light of the world" (John 8:12).
- "I am Alpha and Omega, the beginning and the end. I will give unto him that is athirst of the fountain of the water of life freely" (Rev. 21:6).

☑ *In the list below, place a checkmark before each revelation of Himself in the present that Christ has made known to you.*

☐ *John 8:58*

☐ *John 14:6*

☐ *John 6:51*

☐ *John 11:25*

☐ *John 10:9*

☐ *John 10:11*

☐ *John 8:12*

☐ *Revelation 21:6*

Q: *Which of these aspects of His present reality has meant the most to you? Why?*

____

____

____

____

____

____

____

____

His Glory

When we study the history of God, we learn that God never built a temple that He did not fill with His glory. Do not ask, "*What* is the glory?" but rather ask, "*Who* is the glory?"

> Who being the brightness of his glory, and the express image of his person, and upholding all things by the word of his power, when he had by himself purged our sins, sat down on the right hand of the Majesty on high.
>
> —HEBREWS 1:3

The glory of God is:

- The manifest presence of Christ shining forth through His people.

- The glory of God in the earth.
- The manifestation of resurrection life in His people.

> . . . Christ in you, the hope of glory.
>
> —COLOSSIANS 1:27

Releasing the Glory

To manifest His glory in our temple, God set a process in motion that we might call *surgery.* The Scriptures refer to this divine surgery when they declare:

> For the word of God is quick, and powerful, and sharper than any twoedged sword, piercing even to the dividing asunder of soul and spirit, and of the joints and marrow, and is a discerner of the thoughts and intents of the heart.
>
> —HEBREWS 4:12

The Holy Spirit works to sever the veil between our soul and spirit and allows the manifest presence of Christ to shine forth in our lives.

Homecoming of the Prodigal Church

The redemption and restoration of Ruth included the redemption and restoration of Naomi. Naomi is a type of the present church age that has forsaken the presence of God for tradition, form, and ritual. Presently, this prodigal church is returning to the "House of Bread" even as the world is covered in the darkness of sin. As a result, her light will shine in the darkness as the glory of God is risen upon her.

> Gentiles shall come to thy light, and kings to the brightness of thy rising.
>
> —ISAIAH 60:3

May we as individuals and as the church of Jesus Christ not settle for anything less than entering into our eternal rest in God, which is our divine inheritance. As we continually surrender our lives to God, we are being restored to the eternal purposes of God for His bride in the earth, fulfilling our eternal destiny, as we have seen foreshadowed so beautifully in the life of Ruth.*

Q: *How has this study guide helped you to enter into an eternal rest and realize your inheritance in Christ?*

____

____

____

____

____

____

Q: *Write a prayer asking God to continue to mature you in this redemption, enabling you to be restored to the eternal purposes of God and to fulfill your destiny upon earth.*

CREATION
HOUSE